This Coloring Book
Belongs to:

BE
Strong
AND
Kick
Ass

WAKE UP.
KICK
ASS.
Repeat.

Magic
is
Something
YOU
MAKE

We
RISE
by lifting
others

I can
DO
HARD
things

Fuck
Excuses

I'M A
Powerful
LOVING
Creative
BEING

KEEP
CALM
AND
stay
STRONG

Don't
GIVE UP

Challenges
make
ME
Stronger

Keep
life
Simple

BE NOT
AFRAID
only
Believe

Kindness
IS
YOUR
SUPER
POWER!

You
TOTALLY
Can

www.ingramcontent.com/pod-product-compliance
Lightning Source LLC
Chambersburg PA
CBHW080820220526
45466CB00011BB/3633
9781651837450